THE GIANTS

1986 GIANTS

ROW 1
2, Raul Allegre
5, Sean Landeta
15, Jeff Hostetler
11, Phil Simms
Head Coach Bill Parcells
53, Harry Carson
17, Jeff Rutledge
22, Lee Rouson
23, Perry Williams

ROW 2
24, Ottis Anderson
25, Mark Collins
27, Herb Welch
30, Tony Galbreath
33, George Adams
34, Elvis Patterson
39, Tyrone Davis
43, Terry Kinard
44, Maurice Carthon
46, Greg Lasker
20, Joe Morris

ROW 3
Ron Erhardt
48, Kenny Hill
51, Robbie Jones
52, Pepper Johnson
54, Andy Headen
55, Gary Reasons
56, Lawrence Taylor
57, Byron Hunt
58, Carl Banks
Defensive Coordinator
Bill Belichick

ROW 4
Receivers Coach
Pat Hodgson
59, Brian Johnston
60, Brad Benson
61, Chris Godfrey
63, Karl Nelson
64, Jim Burt
65, Bart Oates
66, William Roberts
67, Billy Ard
Defensive Line Coach
Lamar Leachman

ROW 5
Tight Ends Coach
Mike Pope
78, Jerome Sally
68, Damian Johnson
69, David Jordan
70, Leonard Marshall
73, John Washington
74, Erik Howard
75, George Martin
76, Curtis McGriff
77, Eric Dorsey
Special Teams Coach
Romeo Crennel

ROW 6
Offensive Line Coach
Fred Hoaglin
80, Phil McConkey
81, Stacy Robinson
83, Vince Warren
84, Zeke Mowatt
86, Lionel Manuel
87, Solomon Miller
88, Bobby Johnson
89, Mark Bavaro
Assistant Special Teams
Coach Mike Sweatman
Strength and Conditioning
Coach Johnny Parker

ROW 7
Running Backs Coach
Ray Handley
Field Sec. Mgr. Joe Mansfield
Asst. Film Coord. John Mancuso
Film Coord. Tony Ceglio
Locker Room Mgr. Ed Wagner
Asst. Equip. Mgr. Jim Phelan
Equipment Mgr. Ed Wagner, Jr.
Head Trainer Ronnie Barnes
Trainer Jim Madaleno
Trainer John Johnson
Head Trainer Emeritus
John Dziegiel
Defensive Backfield Coach
Len Fontes

THE GIANTS: SUPER BOWL SEASON

Photographs by JERRY PINKUS

Introduction by FRANK GIFFORD

WILLIAM MORROW AND COMPANY, INC.

New York

Library of Congress Card Number: 87-62055
ISBN: 0-688-07532-0

Printed in the United States of America

First Edition

1 2 3 4 5 6 7 8 9 10

BOOK DESIGN BY MURRAY BELSKY

To Anita, for her patience and understanding
To Evan, my number-one assistant

ACKNOWLEDGMENTS

I would like to thank Lisa Drew, whose enthusiasm was so contagious.

Tom Power for his confidence in me throughout the season.

Ed Croke for his assistance and input with the facts and stats.

Coach Bill Parcells for the access and freedom to shoot important moments.

Wellington Mara and Tim Mara for the privilege of working for a truly class organization.

A special thanks to Frank Gifford for his support and effort in doing the Introduction.

But most important, to the New York Giants football team . . . you made the pictures come to life.

INTRODUCTION

Jerry Pinkus, for the last four years, has been the photographer of the New York Giants. In that capacity, he has also come to know the Giants team and organization as only a family member can. The following collection of Jerry's work and love is a remarkable chronology of this past season. A championship season, the Super Bowl season. You'll meet the stars "up close and personal" as we like to say at ABC, and you'll enjoy once again the memorable season of 1986.

Frank Gifford

"**H**alf Right Wing Motion 74." It was a simple call . . . nothing exotic, nothing sophisticated. Nor was there any urgency in the huddle as Phil Simms barked it out, raising his voice only to the level that was necessary to override the sellout crowd at the Metrodome in Minneapolis.

Occasionally, all quarterbacks will embellish a call with perhaps a simple reminder of the situation. Asking for a little extra time, or maybe reminding a secondary receiver to "stay alive. I might have to get rid of it." In the late afternoon of last November 16, Phil Simms had no reason to add anything to his call. The Metrodome was alive with the electricity of the moment. Both benches were empty, players and coaches lining the sidelines. The crowd of sixty-three thousand was on its collective feet, and countless millions were glued to their television sets.

It was fourth and 17 with a minute and 12 seconds remaining in the game, and the Giants were losing to the Vikings, 20–19. On the preceding play, Simms had been hammered to the carpet by the Vikings' Doug Martin, the loss carrying the Giants all the way back to their own 48-yard line. This would be it. The final opportunity for the 8 and 2 Giants to pull it out.

Half Right Wing Motion 74 is the most basic play in the Giants seventy passing series. It had been put into the Giants offense in training camp the previous July; and it was the basic formation and pass play from which so many other plays could be run. Phil Simms would recall later he had used the play in its pure form perhaps only three times over the entire season. The mechanics of arriving at such a selection was a fascinating exercise in communication. During the time-out called after Doug Martin's sack-ing of Simms on third down, the Giants' offensive brain trust on the sidelines and in the press box had been as busy as a pinball machine. Even as Phil Simms walked to the sideline, head coach Bill Parcells was talking with offensive coordinator Ron Erhardt, who was high overhead with tight ends coach Mike Pope.

Receivers coach Pat Hodgson was at Bill Parcells's side, as was backup quarterback Jeff Rutledge. A desperate situation such as confronted the Giants could have given way to a useless frantic discussion with a less-disciplined coaching staff. Such was not the case. The back and forth, give and take, covered an amazing amount of possibilities. With Bill Parcells orchestrating the decision-making process, several options were discussed and tossed aside. An "82 go" with all receivers "taking it deep" in hopes of a "Hail Mary" reception or a penalty was thrown out; as was a "Double Q," another desperation route with both outside men "taking it deep" and to the flag. Half Right 74 was almost a consensus call. The major plus was that it put three receivers upfield in excess of 20 yards—Stacy Robinson, Phil McConkey, and Bobby Johnson. Pat Hodgson's request for wing motion received affirmation because it would give Phil one more tool as the play developed to determine the Minnesota coverage, a coverage that everyone seemed to agree would be a "three four deep zone."

If it wasn't the three four as the motion man, Phil McConkey, passed behind Simms, he would be able to read the Minnesota change and adjust accordingly. All this discussion and more transpired within the framework of the one-minute time-out.

Now all that remained was the execution. The formation set Stacy Robinson split to the left, Bobby Johnson to the right.

McConkey would open in the left slot and go in motion back to the strong side, where Mark Bavaro was slot right. Bavaro would look for a pick up and then slip into an open area while set back Tony Galbreath would run a circle pattern on the left side. It was a play that had first gone up on the board in July, and now, here in November, it was the desperate choice of all involved to "pull this one out."

Although Phil would have preferred the shotgun because of the noise of the Metrodome, the Giants decided to go from under the center. With the anticipated coverage, the prime receiver figured to be Stacy Robinson. Simms recalls as he moved up to the line of scrimmage after breaking from the huddle that he quietly said to himself, "I'll look right and then come back to Robinson, but don't forget you've always got Bobby." The execution of Half Right Wing Motion 74 took only a few seconds, but it would have a profound impact on the Giants' season. As Simms dropped into the pocket, looked right, and then back to Robinson, he saw that his young receiver had been knocked off stride. Instantly, he looked right again for McConkey who, having read his coverage, was taking it straight downfield looking for the seam in the Minnesota zone. Meanwhile, Bobby Johnson had drawn the expected double coverage on the far outside. As he had done so often in training camp and in practice, Johnson took it upfield some 20 yards and then peeled back to the sideline. It was at that moment that the Vikings' deep cornerback was influenced by the streaking McConkey. As the cornerback eased off Johnson to help his deep safety with McConkey, Simms, now in trouble with the Minnesota pass rush, caught sight of Bobby Johnson's helmet moving back to the sideline and into a clear area. It had to be Johnson, and it had to be now . . . and Simms fired.

Phil Simms never saw the completed pass for the first down at the Vikings' 30-yard line. He was buried as he released the ball. As he looked to the Minnesota sideline, however, he knew the pass was good when he saw the despair expressed by the Vikings' defensive coordinator, Floyd Peters. Three plays later, as time was running out, Raul Allegre ended the series with a 33-yard chip shot, and the Giants had defeated the Vikings, 22–20.

But this was far more than a single victory, this come-from-behind improbable win. In many ways it marked the Giants' transition from a team who felt they could win to a team who knew they could win. They believed in their defense, and they believed in Bill Parcells and his staff, who brought all the components together. But most of all, they believed in themselves. They would not lose again, and the long-sought-after NFL championship and Super Bowl title would become a reality.

For all intents and purposes, the New York Giants' road to the Super Bowl began back on January 5, 1986, in the cramped visitors' locker room at Soldier Field in Chicago. The Giants had just trooped off that wind-whipped field in sub-freezing conditions as 21–0 losers to the Chicago Bears in the divisional playoff game, a game the Bears would use as a springboard to their eventual Super Bowl championship weeks later.

As the Giants were thawing out, heat alone was not sufficient to erase the numbing effects of their shutout loss. But before anger or depression could take over, Bill Parcells mounted a platform in the midst of his players and took advantage of the moment to chart a course for the following year. He told them that they had come a long way, but still had much more to accomplish. He cited areas in which a coordinated and cooperative effort would be mandatory if success were to follow. He mentioned intensity and a dedicated work ethic and he promised his players that if their efforts were put forth with zeal, the club would be even more successful the following season.

Pro Bowl linebacker Harry Carson, a veteran of ten seasons with the team, joined Parcells on the platform. His comments were brief and to the point. "Bill's right on the money," said Carson. "We came up short in a lot of areas today . . . but I'm telling you here and now that this is the best Giants' team I've ever played with and we're not that far away from being the best team in the league. We've got to erase this loss, work our butts off during the off-season, and come together next July in training camp and get it done."

Thus the wheels were set in motion for a extraordinary off-season work program by the Giants, followed by a spirited, yet businesslike, training camp. This set the tone for the best season in club history, a season of team and individual brilliance that carried the team to the NFC East championship, followed by three smashing playoff victories and a first-ever Super Bowl championship.

By mid-March 1986, some ten weeks after the loss to the Bears, the off-season work program began, and nearly forty players were participating. Under the direction of strength and conditioning coach Johnny Parker, the players were at Giants Stadium four days a week, gathering as a team in the weight room and forming bonds and work habits that were to continue throughout the year.

More pieces to the master plan were added in late April during the NFL draft. Already considered to be a defensive-oriented team, the Giants used their first six selections in the draft for more defensive players, and the usual cadre of sceptics scoffed, wondering why, and insisted that the Giants instead needed offensive help. By season's end, however, those six defensive rookies—linemen Eric Dorsey, Erik Howard, and John Washington; defensive backs Mark Collins and Greg Lasker; and linebacker Pepper Johnson—all made key contributions to the overall success of the club.

Mini-camps in May kept the pot boiling as Parcells and his coaching staff laid the groundwork for the regimen that would be followed in the July preseason training camp: work, hard work, followed by more hard work and constant conditioning, and then more conditioning. The team would have fresh legs for the long season and the ability to be strong at the end of the games.

When the training camp began in earnest in July, problems in the offensive backfield surfaced almost immediately. Pro Bowl running back Joe Morris was absent due to contractual differences, and then fullback George Adams, a solid contributor in his rookie year and the projected starter in '86, went down with a pelvic-bone chip injury that was to sideline him for the entire year. Nonetheless, the squad worked on diligently and with unity of purpose.

Eventually, Morris returned to the fold, but not before he had missed the entire training camp and preseason. He finally reached contractual agreement on the afternoon of September 8, just hours before the Giants were to begin the 1986 season with a Monday-night date against the Cowboys in Dallas.

The season began in alarming fashion. With a nationwide audience looking on, the Giants fell into a quick 14–0 hole in the opener, the result of sloppy tackling on defense and a critical fumble on offense. But even in this malaise of mistakes a key trait of the club began to emerge . . . the ability to rally and bounce back from adversity. With Phil Simms firing for 300 yards and three touchdowns, the Giants battled back into a 28–24 lead with less than two minutes to play, only to run out of gas defensively as Dallas stormed back to win the game, 31–28, in the final seconds.

Parcells was hardly in a pleasant mood on the charter flight back home. He was chagrined as much as he was angry, particularly by the defensive performance, and he vowed to achieve instant improvement. The club was 0–1, and looming on the horizon were a pair of AFC West opponents, the San Diego Chargers, who had scored over 50 points in their opening romp over Miami, and an away game with the always formidable Los Angeles Raiders.

To say that the practice sessions after the Dallas setback were intense would be an understatement. Nonetheless, the club responded, and the proud defensive unit, which had surrendered 31 points to the Cowboys, came together again with a vengeance. For the rest of the year, no team would score more than 20 points against them, and in three of their first five victories, the club would not allow a touchdown.

The Chargers were the first to feel the wrath of the rejuvenated defense. After scoring 50-plus points against the Dolphins, the Chargers were shackled to just 265 yards of total offense. Veteran QB Dan Fouts was intercepted five times and the Giants romped to a 20–7 victory as Simms passed for 300 yards for a second straight week.

Next came the long trip to battle the Raiders in Los Angeles, and this time the defense nearly pitched a shutout against Jim Plunkett and the former Super Bowl champions. The Raiders were limited to a trio of field goals, and Plunkett was constantly under pressure, suffering three sacks along the way. Meanwhile, Joe

Morris came up with his first 100-yard rushing game of the season, and second-year tight end Mark Bavaro was a powerhouse receiving and blocking, catching six passes for 106 yards and carrying tacklers on his back like sacks of potatoes.

Parcells was particularly pleased with the way the team again dealt with adversity, this time bouncing back from a 6–0 halftime deficit to win the game, 14–9. Simms fired a pair of second-half touchdown passes, both to WR Lionel Manuel, for the triumph, but the offense also successfully killed the clock in the final 7 minutes with an astute ball-control performance that denied the Raiders a last chance. And winning on the road against a quality team was of paramount importance to the Giants, given the opening-day malfeasance against the Cowboys in Dallas.

Back in Giants Stadium the following week against the much-improved New Orleans Saints, the Giants were faced with yet another challenge that was to prove to be of far-reaching significance. While they had mounted an impressive rally to overcome the tough Raiders the preceding week, the challenge from the Saints may have been even more difficult.

With Joe Morris out of the game because of illness, the Giants also lost their top receiver, Lionel Manuel, with a knee injury that would keep him sidelined for the next twelve weeks. Meanwhile, the Saints had stormed to a 17–0 lead on a 63-yard TD bomb when two of the Giants' defensive backs collided; the other two scores resulted from costly pass interceptions. Undaunted, the Giants showed that comeback power again. The defense strangled the Saints' offense to just 13 yards in the second half, while Simms threw a pair of TD passes, the second of which was a 4-yarder to reserve TE Zeke Mowatt in the final period to cement a 20–17 triumph.

The following two weeks produced two more key victories over NFC East opposition, and in both instances, the defense continued to manhandle opposing offenses. Despite a sputtering attack in St. Louis, the Giants produced a 13–6 victory over the Cardinals on a pair of Raul Allegre field goals and a touchdown dive by Joe Morris. With the offense foundering somewhat, the defense had its second touchdown-shutout, limiting the Birds to a pair of field goals while hounding St. Louis quarterback Neil Lomax from start to finish. All told, Lomax was sacked seven times in the game, twice each by Lawrence Taylor, Carl Banks, and Leonard Marshall.

A week later, the defense continued on the prowl, only this time the offense joined in the attack by rolling up 400 yards of offense en route to a smashing 35–3 romp over Philadelphia. By holding the Eagles wihtout a touchdown, the defense ran its string to 11 consecutive quarters without yielding a touchdown to the opposition. All told the Eagles managed only 117 yards of offense in the game as Lawrence Taylor ran roughshod with nine total tackles and four of the six QB sacks perpetrated on the Philly throwers. And Phil Simms was sharp, completing 20 of 29 passes and a pair of touchdown connections to Solomon Miller and Lee Rouson.

Headed to Seattle with five straight victories in the bank, the Giants nonetheless were faced with a rugged portion of their schedule and would have to get through it without the full firepower of the passing attack. Not only was Lionel Manuel out for twelve weeks, but the other starting WR, Stacy Robinson, had injured an ankle against the Eagles and he would miss the next four weeks. Additionally, WR Bobby Johnson was bothered by a chronic ankle injury, and TE Mark Bavaro had suffered a jaw injury as well as a foot injury; he was playing, but certainly not at full speed.

These weaknesses were felt almost immediately. With Simms experiencing difficulties with the receivers he had, the Seahawks came up with four interceptions, two of which were tipped, and ended the Giants' winning streak with a 17–12 victory in the Kingdome. Both of Seattle's TDs and their FG were the results of those interceptions. Yet the Giants still had one last chance to pull the game out of the fire with a first down at the Seattle 22 and just 2 minutes remaining. Instead, Simms watched as two of his passes into the end zone were bobbled, and the Seahawks held on to win. Afterward in the locker room, Lawrence Taylor was not pleased. The linebacker does not like to lose . . . ever, and he made his feelings known to the rest of the club. ''That was a lousy performance," he bellowed. "We have got to get better, and we better start gettin' it done now."

Joe Morris had rushed for 116 yards in that losing cause, and in the next three weeks, with a crippled array of receivers, Morris would have to bear the brunt of the Giants' offense. The powerful five-foot seven-inch dynamo would do just that.

Back at Giants Stadium the next week against the division-leading Washington Redskins on another Monday night, Morris exploded for a 181-yard rushing effort, pacing the Giants to a 20–3 lead over the Skins midway through the third quarter. But the tough Skins bounced back on a passing onslaught by QB Jay Schroeder to knot the contest at 20–20. Then, Morris took it in his own hands again for the final drive. From the Giants' 44-yard line, Morris first burst off tackle for 34 yards, and added 9 more on his next two carries. Then he swept 13 yards around right end for the touchdown with just 1:44 left to play to give the Giants a crucial 27–20 triumph.

Next came the Cowboys, now involved in a three-way tie for first place in the NFC East with the same 6–2 record as the Giants and Redskins. Morris again rose to the occasion, rushing for 181 yards for a second consecutive game, including a pair of Morris touchdown runs that helped the Giants build a 17–7 lead into the fourth period. When Dallas scored to cut it to 17–14, the defense in general, and veteran defensive end George Martin in particular, took control.

With Dallas in possession and with less than 2 minutes to play, the Cowboys drove to the Giants' 30-yard line. Then Martin, a twelve-year veteran, made three big plays. First, he blew by Cowboy tackle Phil Pozderac to record a 14-yard QB sack. Then he forced Pozderac into a holding penalty that negated a 30-yard pass completion, and finally, he juked Pozderac into a false start penalty that killed another big pass completion. The Cowboys were sizzled, but also cooked, when a last-second 63-yard FG attempt fell far short and the Giants held on for the big 17–14 victory.

Still another murderous portion of the schedule followed. In the next month, the Giants faced three road trips versus Philadelphia, Minnesota, and San Francisco, and their only home game, against the Denver Broncos; all but the Eagles were playoff-contention teams. The Giants had their work cut out for them.

The Eagles, always fierce at home, were just that. With Morris rushing for 111 yards and two touchdowns for his fourth straight 100-plus game, the Giants built a 17–0 lead against Philadelphia as the defense continued to find ways to hammer the Eagles. First, they chased Ron Jaworski out of the game with an injured hand, then they battered Randall Cunningham, his successor, totaling seven QB sacks and two interceptions. The Eagles, however, came back with a pair of fourth-quarter TDs to cut it to 17–14, but their last TD came with just a minute remaining, and that's how it ended as the Giants ran their season mark to 8–2.

The Vikings game was to prove to the Giants that they might be a team of destiny. This one was the proverbial seesaw as the two clubs traded field goals through the first half, with the Giants holding a 9–6 edge. Then, the teams traded leads again in the second half on touchdown passes, with a 19–13 Giants lead, after a Phil Simms 25-yard TD strike to Bobby Johnson, evaporating on a Vikings TD connection and a 20–19 Minnesota advantage. Finally, with less than 2 minutes to play, Simms was sacked on third down all the way back to his own 48-yard line and was faced with the fourth down and 17 to go.

Simms's extraordinary effort, which we've already described, did indeed keep the Giants alive as Bobby Johnson collected the first down at the Vikings' 30-yard line. Shortly thereafter, Raul Allegre won the game, 22–20, with his fifth field goal and with just 15 seconds left on the clock.

This breathtaking triumph seemed hard to top, but the coronary Giants had yet more of these to come.

A week later, back at Giants Stadium, the Denver Broncos rode into town with the same 9–2 record that the Giants now had, and this battle turned out to be yet another barn-burner. Again, there was an exchange of field goals in the early going, but with Denver leading 6–3 and about to score again from the Giants' 13-yard line, a John Elway swing pass into the first was one-handed by defensive end George Martin, who then turned and rumbled 78 yards for a touchdown to put the Giants on top, 10–6, at halftime. For Martin, it was the sixth defensive TD of his illustrious career, an all-time NFL record for defensive linemen.

When Denver tied the game at 16–16 in the final minutes, overtime seemed like a possibility. With less than 2 minutes to play and with a third and 21 confronting him, Simms once again hit Bobby Johnson for a crucial first-down connection to keep a drive alive. With 57 seconds left, Simms found WR Phil McConkey for a 46-yard gain down the middle, and then Allegre booted another game-winning FG, this one from 34 yards, to win it, 19–16, with just 6 seconds left on the clock.

Two straight weeks of palpitations for Giants fans, but a continuing surge of feeling that these Giants players were on a personal crusade and were refusing to lose, no matter how bleak a situation might seem. The drama would continue the following week.

With those back-to-back last-second victories, the Giants went to the West Coast to meet the San Francisco 49ers in their third Monday-night game of the season.

If there were any lingering doubts about the Giants' refusal-to-die mentality, they were completely dispelled on national television in the San Francisco game. With Joe Montana performing like a magician, the Niners roared to a 17–0 halftime lead, and rarely, if ever, do the 49ers lose a lead of that magnitude at Candlestick Park. This was to be the exception to the rule. With Phil Simms pitching perfectly, the Giants stormed back in the third period for a 21-point onslaught, and then the defense throttled the Niners down completely en route to this spine-tingling 21–17 triumph. Simms completed 27 passes for 388 yards in the win, with perhaps the most spectacular play coming from TE Mark Bavaro, who took a 10-yard pass over the middle, then dragged a trio of 49er tacklers another 20 yards for a 31-yard gain that ignited the Giants' offense.

The next stop was in RFK Stadium, Washington, D.C., as the Giants and Redskins squared off for the NFC East title, each with 11–2 marks and both on 5-game winning streaks. Again, the Giants mounted a perfect amalgamation of offense and defense, powering to a 24–7 lead late in the final period before the Skins could score a TD with just 5 minutes to play. Simms threw for three touchdowns in the victory while passing for 265 yards, and the defense hounded Jay Schroeder throughout, sacking him four times and intercepting a season-high six passes . . . by six different defenders. Lawrence Taylor also continued his personal crusade against the Skins, registering five tackles and three of the QB sacks on Schroeder. Taylor also was responsible for most of the pressures that led to Giants interceptions.

When the Redskins were also downed by the Denver Broncos the next week, the Giants clinched the NFC East championship —their first ever—but even with the title flag secured, the team kept the intensity level tuned up. With two regular-season games to go, the Giants wanted the home-field advantage throughout the playoffs, so victories remained important. That being the case, Joe Morris grabbed 179 yards and three touchdowns as the Giants whacked the St. Louis Cardinals, 27–7, with the defense sacking Cards QB Neil Lomax nine times, led by rookie Pepper Johnson's nine tackles and two sacks. A week later, the Giants ended the regular season with a 55–24 rout of the Green Bay Packers to finish at 14–2 and with the home-field advantage well secured. In the finale, Simms threw three touchdown passes, two to Mark Bavaro, and Morris rushed for 115 yards to finish the year with a club record 1,516 yards rushing. Bavaro also finished with an all-time club record for tight ends with 66 catches for 1,001 yards.

That home-field advantage, devastating defense, some Phil Simms passing magic, and weather conditions all merged in the NFC divisional and championship games that followed at Giants Stadium.

With the NFC's number-one rated offensive team, the San Francisco 49ers, as the opening playoff opponent, that Giants' defense reached its pinnacle of power. The defense swarmed all over the 49ers, stuffing their running game to a paltry 29 yards on 20 attempts for a miniscule 1.5 average, while hounding QB Joe Montana to just 8 completions. The Giants intercepted Montana twice, the second of which was returned 34 yards for a touchdown by Lawrence Taylor, and on that play, Montana was crushed by tackle Jim Burt just as he threw and was knocked out of the game with a concussion. The attack continued against backup Jeff Kemp for another interception and sack, and when the final fury had subsided, the Giants had shattered the 49ers, 49–3. Simms needed to complete only nine passes, but four of those were touchdown darts to Mark Bavaro, Phil McConkey, Bobby Johnson, and Zeke Mowatt, and when the Niners got concerned about Simms's radarlike accuracy and dropped off, then Joe Morris stormed inside and outside of defenders for a 159-yard rushing day and two touchdowns of his own. It was the most magnificent display of offensive-defensive dominance of the entire year, and the final margin of victory was the largest in club playoff history.

The following week, with an all-time record 76,633 crowd roaring their support, the Giants won the toss at the start of the NFC championship joust with the Redskins and elected to kick off, thereby taking advantage of wind gusts that ranged from 17 to 25 miles per hour. The strategy paid off immediately.

The defense pounded the Skins on Washington's first two possessions, forcing punts on both occasions, and both punts journeyed less than 30 yards into the swirling winds. Given advantageous field position, the Giants capitalized in both instances, converting a field goal on the first try and a touchdown bullet from Simms to Lionel Manuel on the next for an early 10–0 lead. Then in the next period, playing into the wind, the Giants pounced on a Redskin fumble and slammed home another scoring drive, with Joe Morris slanting in from a yard out for the 17–0 bulge that was to endure for the remainder of the game and make the Giants champions for the first time in many seasons.

For a second straight playoff game, the defense was devastating. Not only were the Redskins held scoreless, but their offense managed just 40 yards rushing and but 150 net yards passing on 50 attempts. Jay Schroeder was sacked four times, intercepted once, and the Skins were, now get this right, 0 for 18 on third- and fourth-down conversions! The fans and players danced in exultation . . . tackle Jim Burt went up into the stands to embrace spectators . . . and the Giants were on their way to the Super Bowl.

The rest is history.

The Giants worked hard and with special fervor during their closed practice sessions at the Los Angeles Rams' complex in Anaheim, California. Years of frustration were being chipped away, piece by piece, and when Super Bowl Sunday dawned warm and clear in Pasadena, the Giants players were ready for combat hours before the scheduled 3:13 P.M. kickoff time.

Denver was formidable, as expected, throughout the first half, but the Giants' defense, while bending on occasion, rose to the challenge with a sinewy goal-line stand that thwarted the Broncos on a first-and-goal situation, and then forced another missed FG attempt on a Denver incursion inside the Giants' 20-yard line. Down 10–9 at halftime, the Giants swarmed back in the second half for 24 unanswered points on the superior performance of Phil Simms, winning the world's championship with ease by a 39–20 final. Simms set an all-time Super Bowl and playoff record with 22 of 25 pass completions for 268 yards and 3 touchdowns, and Bill Parcells's ''fresh legs'' theory proved on the money as his young key reserves pounded on Denver throughout the game and took their eventual toll.

Simms won the Super Bowl Most Valuable Player award, Lawrence Taylor won the NFL's Most Valuable Player laurels, and Parcells was a landslide winner of all the Coach of the Year awards throughout the land.

The real winners, however, with this team of destiny were the millions of Giants fans. The last NFL championship Giants team had been in 1956, when they beat the Chicago Bears, 47–7, in their first year at Yankee Stadium. There would be many other close shots at the illusive title over the next three decades, but on each occasion, just as it would seem that finally everything was coming together, something would happen. There were draft picks that didn't pan out; there were key injuries; always something. But through it all, even though they grumbled, suffered, and at times bitterly expressed their disappointment, Giants fans remained steadfast in their hopes and dreams. They traveled from

Yankee Stadium to the years in isolation at Yale Bowl. They suffered what many thought was the ultimate disgrace when they were beaten by the then much-hated New York Jets in a pre-season game in 1969. And then there was "the Fumble" and the humiliating loss to the Eagles in 1978. Defeat was snatched from the jaws of victory when all that was required was to run out the clock. After that it was almost as though everything that could go wrong had gone wrong.

The following year the turnaround began, and it began with the hiring of a rotund philosophical football man named George Young. And a good argument could be made that this was what set the Giants on the road to the Super Bowl. A former player, a former coach, and an unlikely scholar with a pair of masters degrees from Johns Hopkins and Loyola College, George Young was the right man for the right job at the right time.

In January 1987, I sat with George just prior to the kickoff of Super Bowl XXI. Looking down on the Rose Bowl field as the Giants and Broncos warmed up, I couldn't help but remark to George, "How proud you must feel." Ever the worrier, George didn't quite get it. He mumbled something to the effect, "We'll see, we'll see."

What George didn't understand was that I was not referring to the Super Bowl game that was coming up or, for that matter, to the outcome of it. I was simply hitting on the obvious, and that is what a remarkable job he had done in his eight years as a Giant. It was his team in almost every respect. True, Bill Parcells is now most certainly one of the top coaches in the game, but it took a George Young to recognize that following the sudden and unexpected departure of Ray Perkins in 1982, giving Parcells the top job would allow the Giants ship to change captains with hardly a ripple; and the process of building the Giants that began with Young's first draft choice in 1979, Phil Simms, continued right on schedule.

The total commitment to the course set by George Young was also shared by the members of the Giants management. Co-owners Wellington and Tim Mara have had their much-publicized differences in the past, but no one who has ever been associated with them could ever doubt that their mutual goal has been to develop the best football team possible.

The Maras are a very private family and proud of their heritage in the National Football League; and even though there have been other NFL championships over the Giants' long and storied history, their first Super Bowl title had to have been the sweetest of them all. During the course of the Giants' victory over the Denver Broncos, Wellington and Tim, as well as the rest of the Mara family, certainly had cause to reflect back over the sixty-two-year history of the franchise and savor what was happening. It's a matter of economic record that the scalping price of a pair of Super Bowl XXI tickets would have been enough to purchase the franchise back in 1925. That was the year in which the family patriarch, the late Timothy J. Mara, took a "flier," so to speak, and joined a band of teams that called themselves the National Professional Football League.

There would be great moments for the Maras over the years. There would be championship teams and there would be years in which there would be tremendous economic pressure merely to survive.

Of considerable pride to me is that I have known all the Maras of the New York Giants. My first contract as a number-one draft pick back in 1952 would be an embarrassment in light of today's "zeros." It wasn't for me, however, and I'll never forget the thrill of signing my name right over the names of Timothy's sons, Wellington Mara, secretary, and John V. Mara, president.

Later, John's son Tim Mara would become the dear and trusted friend who I first met playing Ping-Pong as a sixteen-year-old in my first training camp at St. Peter, Minnesota. There would be many other contracts, some of them I don't think I even signed. There would be an agreement, a handshake; and there was never a question in my mind that the agreement would be honored, whether the contract was signed or not. That relationship has, of course, disappeared with agents, lawyers, and tax brackets. What has not disappeared, even in an era of spiraling franchise values, is the honesty, integrity, and character of the ownership and players of the Super Bowl champion New York Giants.

The disappointment of losing in the playoffs to the eventual Super Bowl champion for the third time in five years made the players realize how close they had come to their dream of playing in the Super Bowl.

Damian Johnson participates in the off-season strengthening program.

Leonard Marshall does some abdominal twists to strengthen his trunk muscles.

Training camp marks the start of the season.

Left to right, Head Coach Bill Parcells, Lawrence Taylor, and Defensive Coordinator Bill Belichick have a pre-practice discussion.

Carl Banks takes a welcome break during the twice-a-day practices.

Harry Carson spends a moment
with his daughter before the
Atlanta preseason game.

Left to right, Receivers Coach Pat Hodgson,
Offensive Coordinator Ron Erhardt,
and Coach Bill Parcells view practice
with watchful eyes.

Cowboys 31, Giants 28

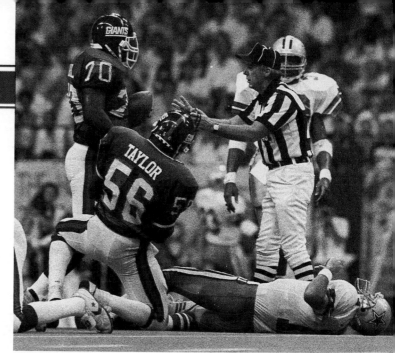

Danny White was sacked by Leonard Marshall (70) for a loss of 12 yards.

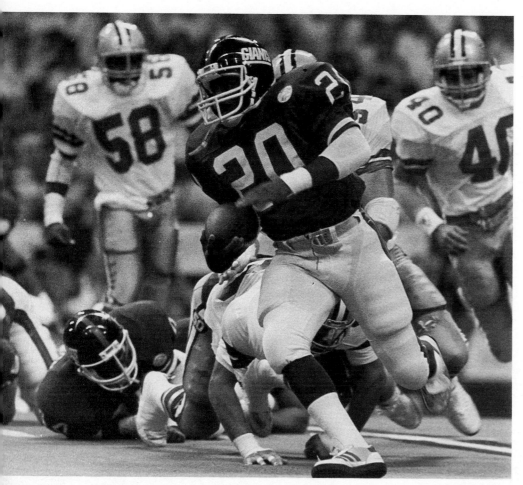

Joe Morris cuts over the left side for a gain of 34 yards.

Joe Morris tries the right side for minus 5 yards as he is tackled by John Dutton.

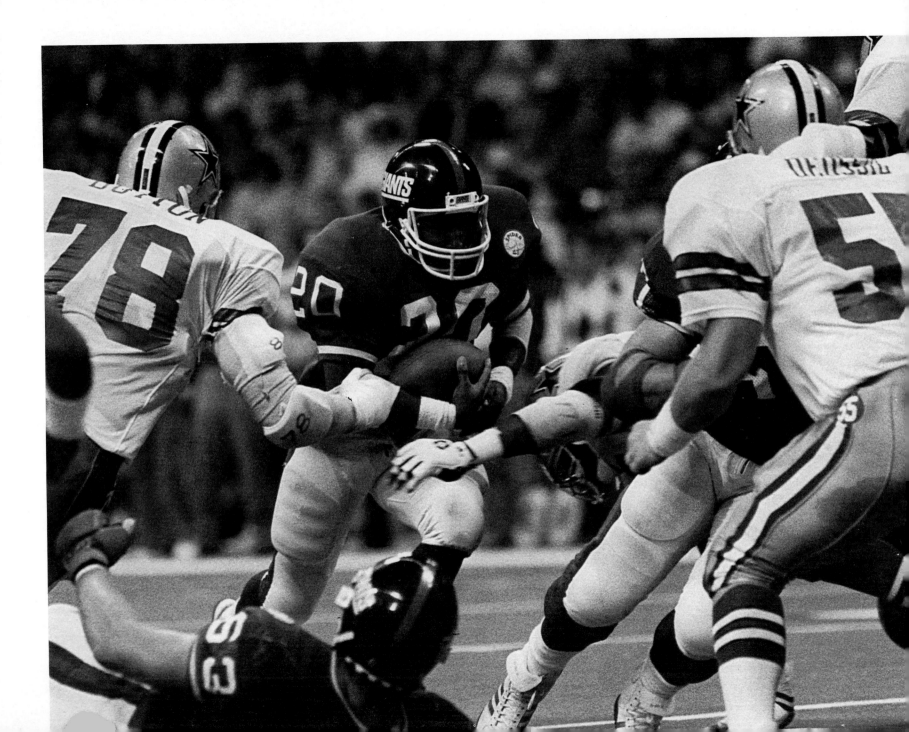

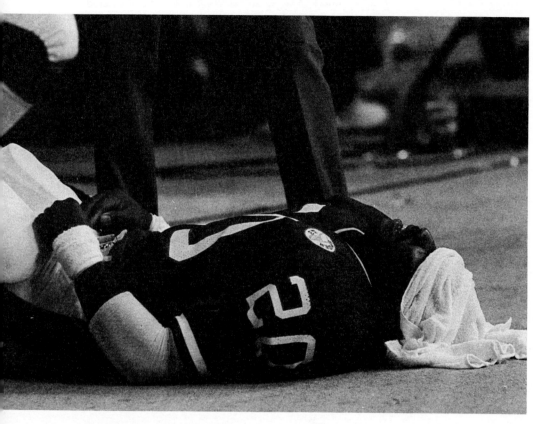

Joe Morris takes a breather after scoring a
2-yard TD, putting the Giants ahead, 21–17.

Phil Simms's pass for Lionel Manuel was dropped.

Former USFL backfield members Herschel Walker and
Maurice Carthon renew their friendship after the game.

Giants 20, San Diego 7

Coach Bill Parcells (right) and the team await the pregame introduction.

Phil Simms hands off to Joe Morris for a 1-yard gain.

Joe Morris went over the right guard for a 1-yard TD.

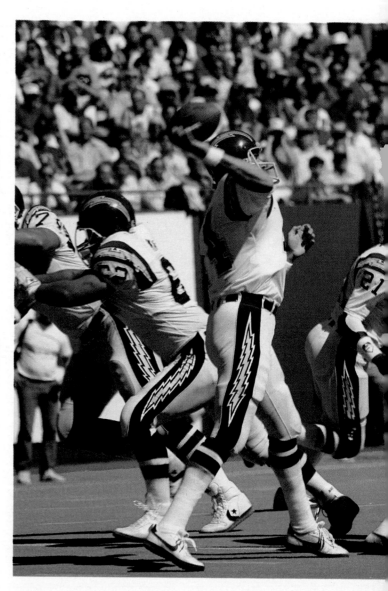

Dan Fouts's (14) pass attempt went incomplete.

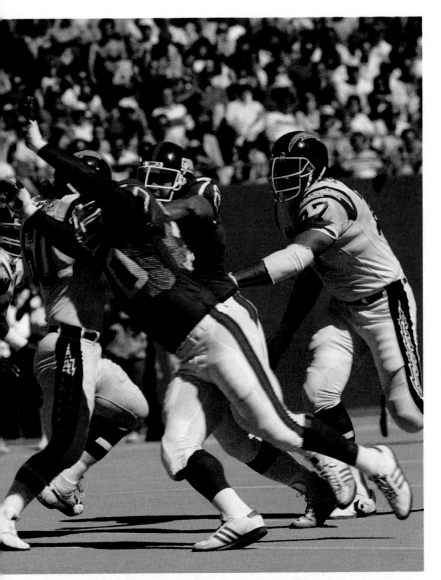

Sean Landeta's punt was downed at the Giant 48-yard line.

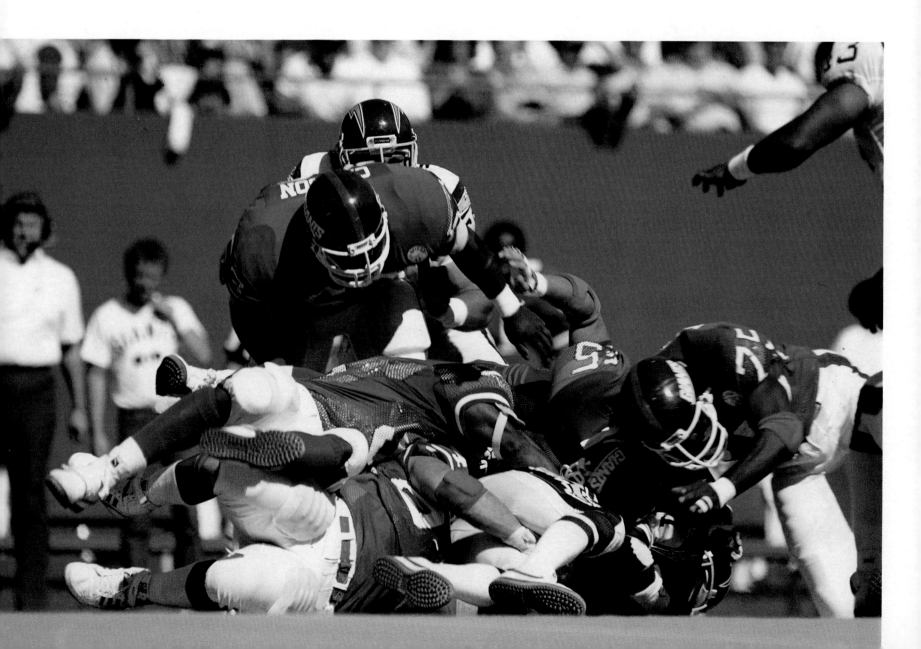

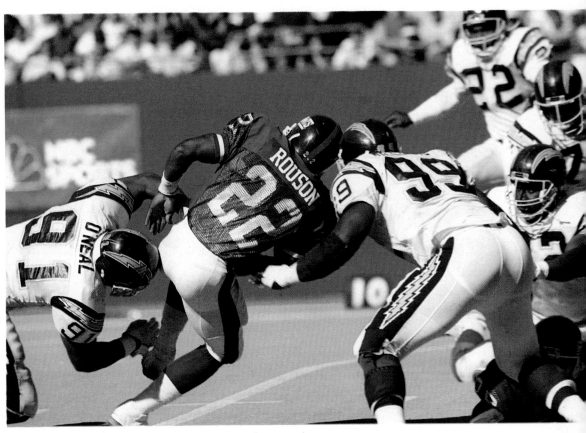

Dan Fouts's pass for Chandler was
intercepted by Terry Kinard.

Lee Rouson tries going over the right guard for no gain.

Gary Anderson tried left end and gained 1 yard.

Giants 14, L.A. Raiders 9

Running back
Joe Morris

Joe Morris
scoots around
the right tackle
for a gain
of 6 yards.

It's first and goal to go from the 1. Lawrence Taylor stops John Elway for a 1-yard loss.

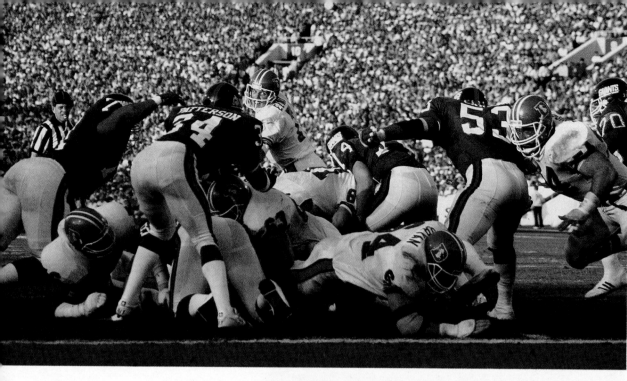

Gerald Willhite tries going up
the middle . . . no gain as
Harry Carson makes the stop.

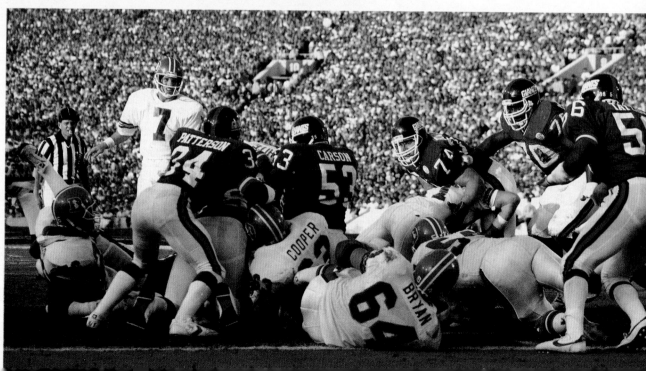

Phil Simms hands off to Maurice Carthon who goes up the middle for a gain of 1 yard.

John Elway is sacked for a loss of 13
yards . . . and a safety by George Martin.

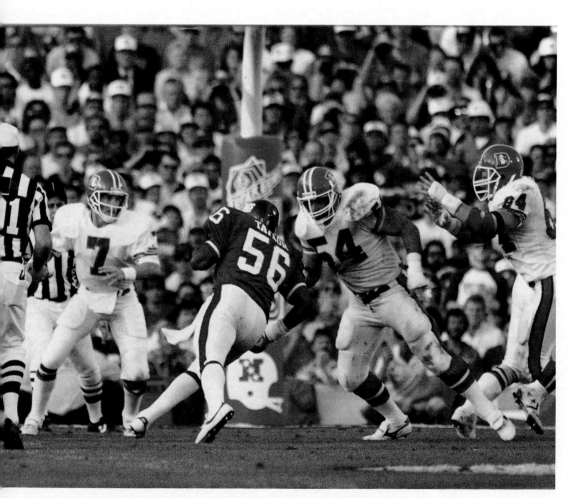

John Elway (7) eyes LT (56) coming after him, but
it was Leonard Marshall who sacked him for a 2-yard loss.

John Elway passed to Gerald Willhite for an 11-yard gain before being brought down by LT.

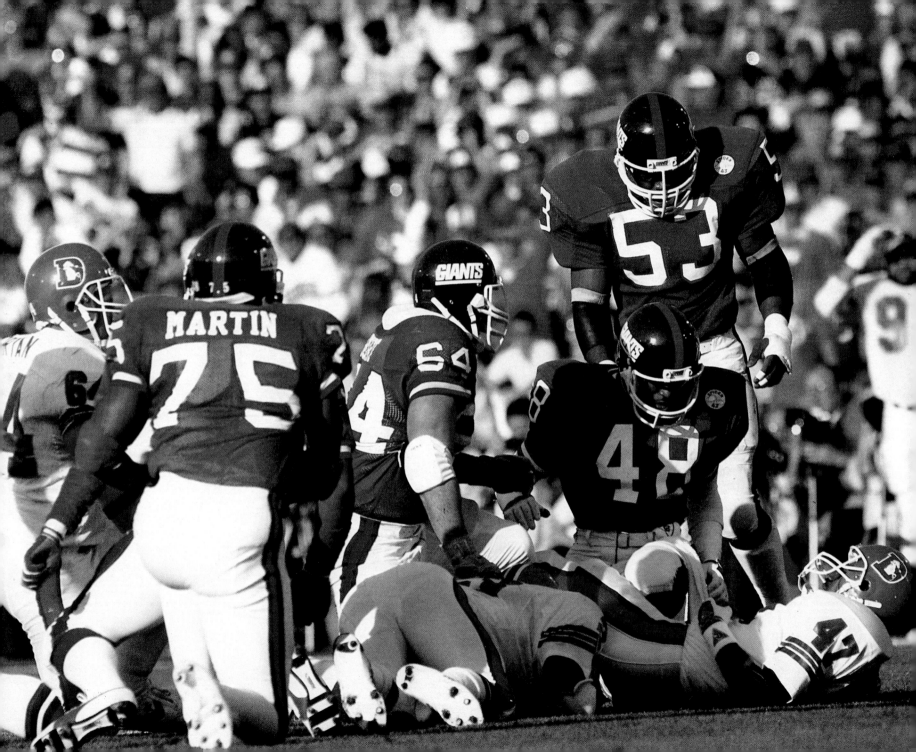

Mark Bavaro makes a 13-yard touchdown reception and gives thanks.

Another pass from Elway to Willhite (47) is incomplete.

Gene Lang (33) returns the kickoff and is stopped by Byron Hunt (57) after a 13-yard return to the Denver 14.

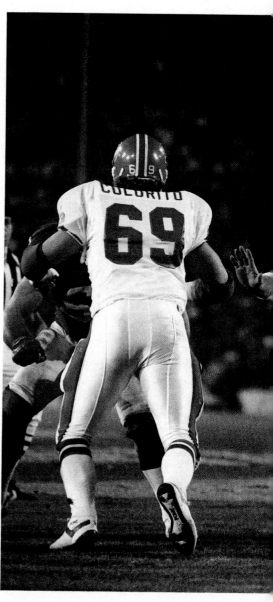

Phil Simms goes back to pass and completes a

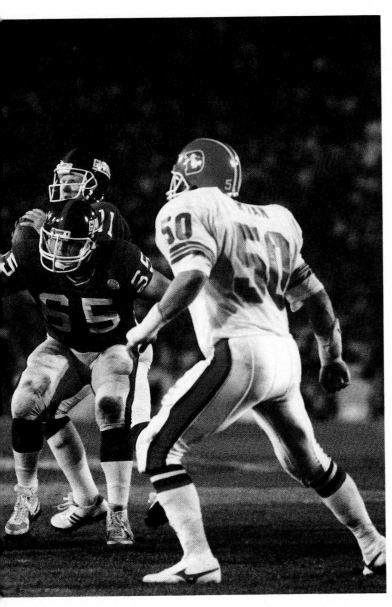

9-yarder to Lionel Manuel.

Phil Simms goes back to pass then runs for a gain of 5 yards.

Denver downs the ball in the end zone for a touchback.

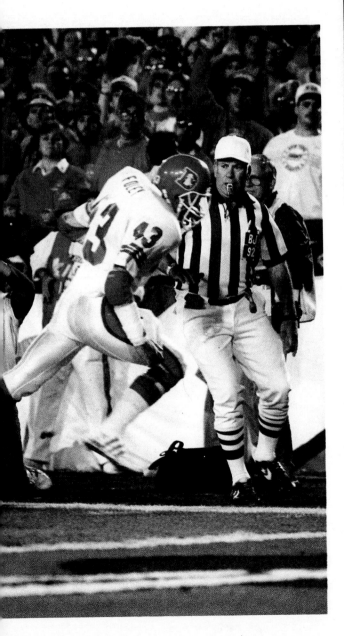

Phil Simms passes to Phil McConkey (80), who goes airborne and lands on the 1-yard line for a gain of 44 yards, but he is 1 yard short of a Super Bowl touchdown.

Phil Simms calls the signals and prepares to hand off to Joe Morris for a sweep wide right and a touchdown.

It's a touchdown for Phil McConkey as he catches a ball off Mark Bavaro.

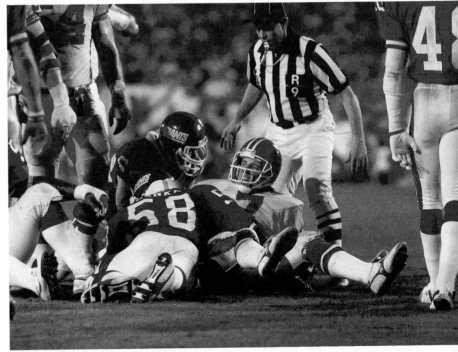

Carl Banks (58) stops John Elway after a 2-yard run.

Phil Simms, Super Bowl MVP, set the following Super Bowl records:
- Most consecutive completions in a game—10
- Highest completion percentage in a game—88.0
- His completion percentage was the highest not only for a Super Bowl game but for any of the 213 postseason games in NFL history (minimum: 15 completions). Phil also holds the Giants record for the most 300-yard games in a career—15.

Joe Morris has another record-setting year:
- Second time All-Pro
- Most yards rushing in a season—1,516
- Most rushing attempts in a season—341
- Most games with 100 yards rushing in a career—16
- Most games with 100 yards rushing in a season—8
- Highest rushing average in a career—4.35
- Most rushing touchdowns in a career—40

LT is interviewed by Irv Cross after the victory. LT honors:
- Sixth time All-Pro
- Most quarterback sacks in a season—20.5
- National Football League Defensive Player of the Year

Commissioner Pete Rozelle (far left) presents the trophy to team president
Wellington Mara (2nd from left) as Brent Musburger of CBS Sports and Coach Bill Parcells look on.

As the team arrives back at the hotel, they are greeted by a swarm of jubilant fans.

Harry Carson has finally had his dream come true.

Team president Wellington Mara is all smiles as he sports his Super Bowl XXI 1987 World Champs hat.

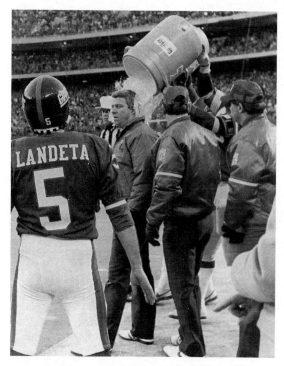

The most anticipated part of a Giants
victory: the ceremonial Gatorade bath

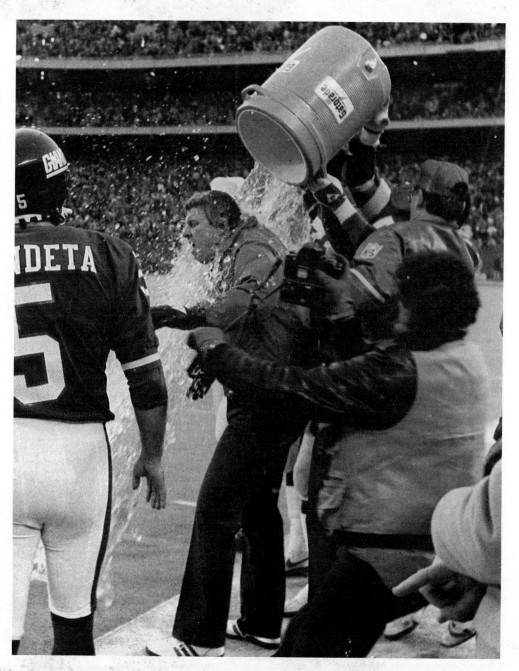